KKB Books
KEEPING KIDS BUSY

COPYRIGHT © 2019 SMALL PUBLISHING LTD

Cover image used under licence from Vecteezy

First published in 2019 by Small Publishing Ltd. All Rights Reserved. No part of this publication may be reproduced, stored in a retrieval system or transmitted in any form or by any means, electronic, mechanical, photocopying, recording or otherwise without the prior permission of the publisher.

WOULD YOU RATHER...

Would You Rather is a great game for getting a conversation started - whether between friends, family or classmates. Just open the book and ask a question! The only rule is that you <u>have to choose</u> between the two options and explain your choice. You are not allowed to respond "both" or "neither". There are no winners or losers. It's all just good fun!

Parents:
Use this book to prompt conversations with the kids without pressure! There will be much giggling involved as they build their confidence and work on skills such as reading aloud, critical and logical thinking, vocabulary, conversation, empathy and debate. Some of the questions will make them think about their values and morals; others will just make them laugh. And of course they will enjoy asking you questions and learning all about what makes you tick, too!

Teachers:
These questions make fabulous writing prompts! In fact we've designed the book so that you can photocopy a page and cut out the 2 questions to hand around the class. They make fun ice-breakers and warm-ups too.

Kids:
We bet you don't know as much about your friends as you think you do! Take turns to ask each other questions and find out...

HOW TO USE THIS BOOK...

Work through the book or open a page randomly. Remember, you have to choose (you can't answer "both" or "neither") and you should explain your choice!

With 2 people:
Player 1 reads aloud the first question and challenges Player 2 to answer it, then hands the book over. Player 2 then reads aloud the second question and Player 1 has to answer.

In a group:
Take turns reading aloud a question. Each member of the group answers, one by one. You can choose to vote on the best answer if you like, or just enjoy listening to them.

Try Not to Laugh Challenge:
Play as above but this time make your answers as outrageous and funny as possible. The aim is to make the other player / players laugh!

In the classroom:
Use the questions as above as an ice-breaking activity. Alternatively use questions as writing prompts; ask the whole class to write their answer down and then perhaps read them out loud to their classmates. How about giving one as a fun homework assignment or holiday activity?

WOULD YOU RATHER...

...have pie in your face

OR

a bucket of water poured over your head?

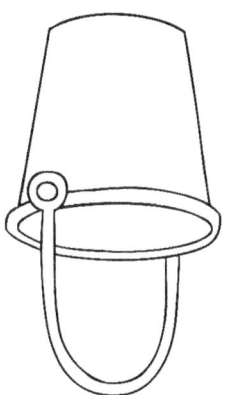

WOULD YOU RATHER...

...be given a cow

OR

5 magic beans?

WOULD YOU RATHER...

...wake up on a desert island

OR

open your eyes to find yourself on a magic carpet?

WOULD YOU RATHER...

...ride a giraffe

OR

ride a kangaroo?

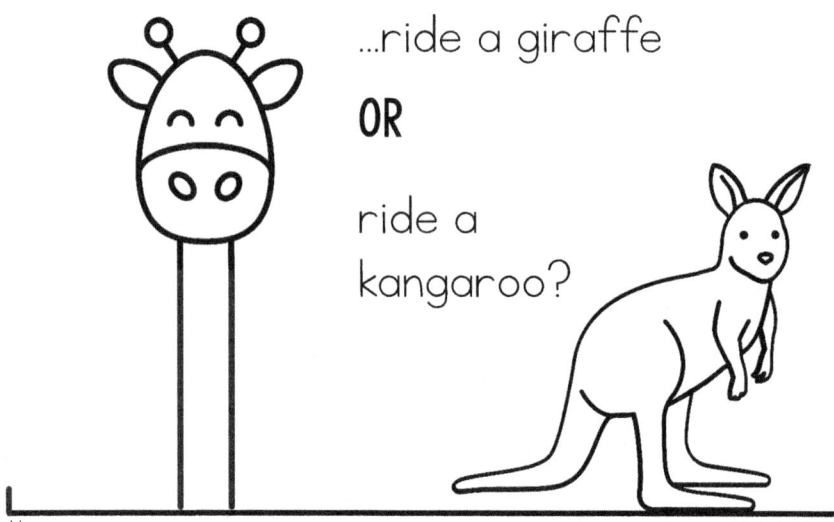

WOULD YOU RATHER...

...run faster than a cheetah

OR

swim like a dolphin?

WOULD YOU RATHER...

...meet a giant

OR

a fairy?

WOULD YOU RATHER...

...climb a mountain

OR

sail an ocean?

WOULD YOU RATHER...

...eat spaghetti with chocolate sauce

OR

ice-cream with ketchup?

WOULD YOU RATHER...

...be a doctor

OR

a dentist?

WOULD YOU RATHER...

...go to school in your underwear

OR

sing a song to someone you've never met?

WOULD YOU RATHER...

...be a pirate

OR

the captain of a cruise ship?

WOULD YOU RATHER...

...trick

OR

treat?

WOULD YOU RATHER...

...travel on a spaceship to Mars

OR

live under the sea for a year?

WOULD YOU RATHER...

...color a picture

OR

recite a poem?

WOULD YOU RATHER...

...meet a dragon

OR

a mermaid?

WOULD YOU RATHER...

...not be able to speak

OR

not be able to read?

WOULD YOU RATHER...

...look for a needle in a haystack

OR

search for a four-leaf clover?

WOULD YOU RATHER...

...be furry

OR

have scales?

WOULD YOU RATHER...

...own a pet lion

OR

a pet elephant?

WOULD YOU RATHER...

...be able to eat all the ice-cream you every want

OR

invent a new ice-cream flavour?

WOULD YOU RATHER...

...meet a vampire

OR

a werewolf?

WOULD YOU RATHER...

...be able to talk to animals

OR

fly by flapping your arms?

Well hello there!

WOULD YOU RATHER...

...eat nothing but meat for a week

OR

exist on nothing but fruit and veg for a week?

WOULD YOU RATHER...

...yawn every time your teacher speaks

OR

giggle every time your teacher walks in the room?

WOULD YOU RATHER...

...have an invisibility cloak

OR

a talking dog?

WOULD YOU RATHER...

...be a spy when you grow up

OR

have so much money that you will never have to work?

WOULD YOU RATHER...

...meet an alien

OR

a robot?

WOULD YOU RATHER...

...act in a horror movie

OR

a fairy tale?

WOULD YOU RATHER...

...make someone cry every time you laugh

OR

make someone laugh every time you cry?

WOULD YOU RATHER...

...have a laugh like a hyena

OR

a giggle like a goat?

WOULD YOU RATHER...

...play a video game on your own

OR

play a soccer game outside with friends?

WOULD YOU RATHER...

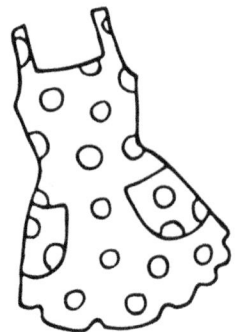

...wear stripes

OR

dots?

WOULD YOU RATHER...

...write a story

OR

read a book?

WOULD YOU RATHER...

...be too hot

OR

too cold?

WOULD YOU RATHER...

...make someone sneeze every time you burp

OR

make someone burp every time you sneeze?

WOULD YOU RATHER...

...live in a tree-house

OR

a log cabin?

WOULD YOU RATHER...

...put your foot into a boot full of spiders

OR

be stung by 3 bees?

WOULD YOU RATHER...

...have a donkey's ears

OR

a dog's tail?

WOULD YOU RATHER...

...wear warm fluffy slippers

OR

summer sandals?

WOULD YOU RATHER...

Who are you looking at?

...click your fingers to go invisible

OR

be able to stretch like rubber?

WOULD YOU RATHER...

...be a famous pop star

OR

a movie actor?

WOULD YOU RATHER...

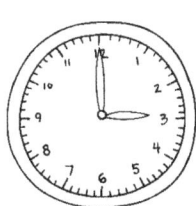

...be able to stop time

OR

speed it up?

WOULD YOU RATHER...

...grow older

OR

or younger for the next three birthdays?

WOULD YOU RATHER...

...build a sandcastle on the beach

OR

a den at the bottom of the garden?

WOULD YOU RATHER...

...talk to a frog

OR

chat with a lizard?

Lovely weather today, isn't it?

WOULD YOU RATHER...

...walk blindfolded through a forest

OR

swim in a sea where there might be sharks?

WOULD YOU RATHER...

...become a teacher

OR

a vet when you grow up?

WOULD YOU RATHER...

...be able to see behind closed doors

OR

listen to conversations in the next door room?

WOULD YOU RATHER...

...find yourself at the top of a lighthouse in the ocean

OR

in a tunnel deep underground?

WOULD YOU RATHER...

...be a pizza cook

OR

a birthday cake baker?

WOULD YOU RATHER...

...answer every question truthfully

OR

answer every question with a lie?

WOULD YOU RATHER...

...discover a new planet

OR

come up with a cure for a deadly disease?

WOULD YOU RATHER...

...be a king or queen of a wonderful kingdom

OR

a superhero?

WOULD YOU RATHER...

...give up everything with sugar in it for a year

OR

lose your pocket money for 12 months?

WOULD YOU RATHER...

...enjoy the snow

OR

spend a day at the beach?

WOULD YOU RATHER...

...everyone always laughed at your jokes

OR

your singing voice always made people cry with joy?

WOULD YOU RATHER...

...dance every time you hear music

OR

stand on your head every time someone sings?

WOULD YOU RATHER...

...drive a truck

OR

ride a bicycle?

WOULD YOU RATHER...

...bounce on a trampoline

OR

swing on a swing?

WOULD YOU RATHER...

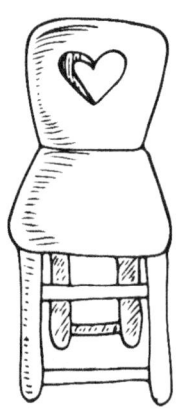

...be a table

OR

a chair?

WOULD YOU RATHER...

...be a hippo

OR

a rhino?

WOULD YOU RATHER...

...have 20 fingers

OR

20 toes?

WOULD YOU RATHER...

...eat nothing but pizza for a whole year

OR

eat nothing but burgers for the next 12 months?

WOULD YOU RATHER...

...be a wizard

OR

an elf?

WOULD YOU RATHER...

...have slinkies for arms

OR

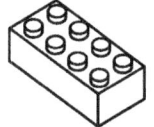

building bricks for toes?

WOULD YOU RATHER...

...be a wasp

OR

a bumble bee?

WOULD YOU RATHER...

...have a green face

OR

grow purple hair?

WOULD YOU RATHER...

...swim with a dolphin

OR

meet your favorite movie star?

WOULD YOU RATHER...

...go scuba diving

OR

explore the rain forest?

WOULD YOU RATHER...

...go on a safari

OR

on a trip around Europe's museums?

WOULD YOU RATHER...

...climb the Eiffel Tower

OR

watch the Changing of the Guard at Buckingham Palace?

WOULD YOU RATHER...

...speak 10 languages

OR

be a math genius?

WOULD YOU RATHER...

...live in an igloo

OR

a cave?

WOULD YOU RATHER...

...go to summer camp

OR

on a holiday to a country you've never visited before?

WOULD YOU RATHER...

...discover a mummy's tomb

OR

crack the code of an ancient language?

WOULD YOU RATHER...

...live in a castle in Scotland

OR

a penthouse in New York?

WOULD YOU RATHER...

...eat only with a spoon

OR

only with a fork?

WOULD YOU RATHER...

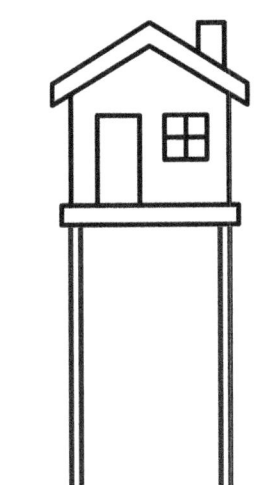

...live in a glass house

OR

a wooden house on stilts?

WOULD YOU RATHER...

...be spaghetti

OR

meatballs?

WOULD YOU RATHER...

...be a musical genius

OR

a mathematical prodigy?

WOULD YOU RATHER...

...travel to the future

OR

live in your chosen period in the past?

WOULD YOU RATHER...

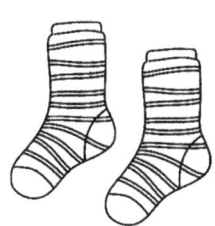

...never wear shoes

OR

never wear socks?

WOULD YOU RATHER...

...mow the lawn

OR

wash the car?

WOULD YOU RATHER...

...go on a TV game show and win the biggest prize

OR

win a contract to star in a new TV series?

WOULD YOU RATHER...

...be the President

OR

an astronaut?

WOULD YOU RATHER...

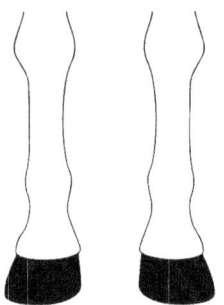

...have snakes for hair

OR

a horse's legs?

WOULD YOU RATHER...

...meet a ghost

OR

an monster?

WOULD YOU RATHER...

...be only able to whisper

OR

only able to shout?

WOULD YOU RATHER...

...be a superhero

OR

a super-villain?

WOULD YOU RATHER...

...lose your sense of smell for a week

OR

lose your sense of taste for 7 days and nights?

WOULD YOU RATHER...

...only be able to speak in rhyme

OR

never be able to say more than 3 words in one sentence?

WOULD YOU RATHER...

...meet a leprechaun

OR

a dinosaur?

WOULD YOU RATHER...

...tickle a tarantula

OR

grapple with a gorilla?

WOULD YOU RATHER...

...play with a puppy

OR

try out a new video game?

WOULD YOU RATHER...

...read the book

OR

watch the movie?

WOULD YOU RATHER...

...have green teeth for a day

OR

fluorescent hair for a week?

WOULD YOU RATHER...

...be trapped in a room with 10 deadly snakes for 10 minutes

OR

go into a lion's cage when it's feeding time?

I've been working up my appetite...

WOULD YOU RATHER...

...meet a bear in the wild

OR

confront a crocodile face to face?

WOULD YOU RATHER...

...have an itch that you can't scratch

OR

always have a small pebble in your shoe?

WOULD YOU RATHER...

...be friends with the most popular kids

OR

with the smartest kids?

WOULD YOU RATHER...

...wake up in the desert

OR

in the jungle?

WOULD YOU RATHER...

...have a teacher you dislike but get all A's

OR

have a teacher you love but get all C's?

WOULD YOU RATHER...

...be good at lots of different things

OR

excel at one particular thing?

WOULD YOU RATHER...

...go to school with mismatched shoes

OR

with your pants on backwards?

WOULD YOU RATHER...

...be a brilliant, rich scientist

OR

a world-famous painter with no money?

WOULD YOU RATHER...

have a small part in a really good movie

OR

be the star in a really bad movie?

WOULD YOU RATHER...

...have to say out loud everything that you are thinking

OR

never say anything again?

WOULD YOU RATHER...

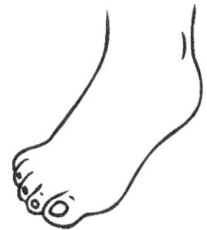

...lick your best friend's foot (yuk)

OR

have him or her lick your foot (yuk)?

WOULD YOU RATHER...

...have lots of energy

OR

lots of money?

WOULD YOU RATHER...

...sleepwalk

OR

sleep talk?

WOULD YOU RATHER...

...be a detective

OR

a firefighter?

WOULD YOU RATHER...

...travel in time to meet your great great grandparents

OR

your great great grandchildren?

WOULD YOU RATHER...

...own a pet porcupine

OR

a pet skunk?

WOULD YOU RATHER...

...be strong

OR

fast?

WOULD YOU RATHER...

...live on a submarine

OR

a spaceship?

WOULD YOU RATHER...

...have a bedroom shaped like a triangle

OR

a bedroom shaped like a circle?

WOULD YOU RATHER...

...have a suit of armor

OR

a horse?

WOULD YOU RATHER...

...be extremely funny

OR

amazingly smart?

WOULD YOU RATHER...

...it was Christmas day

OR

your birthday?

WOULD YOU RATHER...

...stay up really late

OR

wake up really early?

WOULD YOU RATHER...

...be huge

OR

tiny?

WOULD YOU RATHER...

...own a robot

OR

a dinosaur?

WOULD YOU RATHER...

...meet the hero of your favorite book

OR

meet its author?

WOULD YOU RATHER...

...have as much chocolate as you want for the rest of you life

OR

be given $1 million dollars now?

WOULD YOU RATHER...

...your house was surrounded by water

OR

that it sits in the middle of a jungle?

WOULD YOU RATHER...

...forget who you are

OR

forget who everyone else is?

WOULD YOU RATHER...

...have hands instead of feet

OR

...feet instead of hands?

WOULD YOU RATHER...

...have a nose like a carrot

OR

a nose like an apple?

WOULD YOU RATHER...

...live in a home with no electricity for a month

OR

a home with no running water for the same time?

WOULD YOU RATHER...

...hug a panda

OR

a penguin?

WOULD YOU RATHER...

...be the oldest

OR

the youngest sibling in a family with 6 children?

1 2 3 4 5 6 ?

WOULD YOU RATHER...

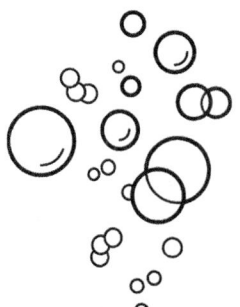

...be able to walk through fire

OR

breathe underwater?

WOULD YOU RATHER...

...be a dog

OR

a cat for a day?

WOULD YOU RATHER...

...have no knees

OR

no elbows?

WOULD YOU RATHER...

...play in a band

OR

in a team?

WOULD YOU RATHER...

...snort like a pig when you laugh

OR

hee-haw like a donkey?

WOULD YOU RATHER...

...eat cabbage and banana stew

OR

eat pickle and pineapple pie?

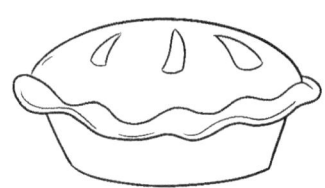

WOULD YOU RATHER...

...have lots of money and few friends

OR

lots of friends and little money?

WOULD YOU RATHER...

...ride a roller-coaster

OR

a ghost train?

WOULD YOU RATHER...

...see a volcano erupt

OR

feel an earthquake?

WOULD YOU RATHER...

...be a wolf

OR

a tiger?

WOULD YOU RATHER...

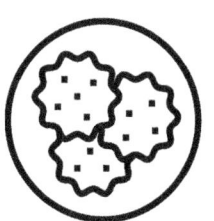

...smell fresh bread

OR

cookies?

WOULD YOU RATHER...

...have a watermelon

OR

a water pistol?

WOULD YOU RATHER...

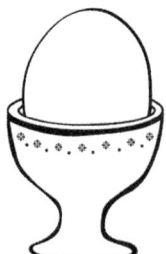

...eat green ham

OR

green eggs?

WOULD YOU RATHER...

...own a lightsabre

OR

have laser eyes?

WOULD YOU RATHER...

...have 10 treats today

OR

20 treats next week?

WOULD YOU RATHER...

...lose your way

OR

lose your marbles?

WOULD YOU RATHER...

...tell funny jokes

OR

listen to scary stories?

WOULD YOU RATHER...

...make a new friend

OR

keep an old one?

WOULD YOU RATHER...

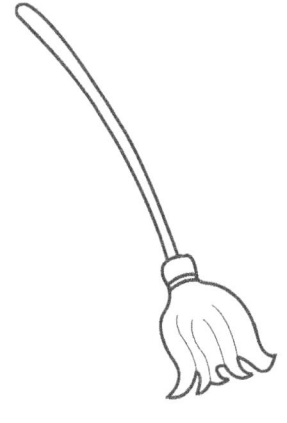

...be chased by a giant vacuum cleaner

OR

run away from a giant broomstick?

WOULD YOU RATHER...

...be scared of the dark

OR

afraid of creepy crawlies?

WOULD YOU RATHER...

...be a cartoon character

OR

a character in a story book?

WOULD YOU RATHER...

...be a fruit

OR

a vegetable?

WOULD YOU RATHER...

...be made out of chocolate

OR

be made out of apple sauce?

WOULD YOU RATHER...

...receive gifts

OR

give gifts?

WOULD YOU RATHER...

...go to a friend's party

OR

throw a party of your own?

WOULD YOU RATHER...

...live 80 years in the future

OR

live 80 years in the past?

WOULD YOU RATHER...

...give praise

OR

be praised?

WOULD YOU RATHER...

...engage a stranger in conversation

OR

not say one word in 6 hours?

WOULD YOU RATHER...

...meet a centaur

OR

encounter a unicorn?

WOULD YOU RATHER...

...eat cake for breakfast

OR

munch on cornflakes for supper?

WOULD YOU RATHER...

...ask a question

OR

answer a question?

WOULD YOU RATHER...

...be the best

OR

be the kindest?

WOULD YOU RATHER...

...learn to drive

OR

learn to fly?

WOULD YOU RATHER...

..visit the zoo

OR

help the animals escape?

WOULD YOU RATHER...

...chat with a mouse

OR

gossip with a rabbit?

WOULD YOU RATHER...

...enjoy a barbecue

OR

indulge in a picnic?

WOULD YOU RATHER...

...be a marshmallow

OR

a jelly bean?

WOULD YOU RATHER...

...share a see-saw with a buffalo

OR

balance with a bumblebee?

WOULD YOU RATHER...

...play a trick on a friend

OR

learn a magic trick?

WOULD YOU RATHER...

...visit an amusement park

OR

take a trip to the best library in the world?

WOULD YOU RATHER...

...left

OR

right?

WOULD YOU RATHER...

...eat your greens

OR

take your medicine?

WOULD YOU RATHER...

...meet a Tyrannosaurus Rex

OR

a dodo?

WOULD YOU RATHER...

...meet an angry skunk

OR

a hungry shark?

What's for dinner?

WOULD YOU RATHER...

...play chess against your teacher

OR

challenge your oldest family member?

WOULD YOU RATHER...

...have a bath full of baked beans

OR

a shower with spaghetti hoops?

WOULD YOU RATHER...

...be famous for your looks

OR

well-known your deeds?

WOULD YOU RATHER...

...live in an ice age

OR

during the Jurassic period?

WOULD YOU RATHER...

...learn to play a banjo

OR

a didgeridoo?

WOULD YOU RATHER...

...cook every meal for a week

OR

do all the cleaning up after meals for the same period?

WOULD YOU RATHER...

...find a dragon in your back yard

OR

discover a mischievous gnome under your bed?

WOULD YOU RATHER...

...meet Jack (from Jack and the Beanstalk)

OR

Hansel (from Hansel and Gretel)?

WOULD YOU RATHER...

...have a dog named Wolf

OR

a wolf named Dog?

WOULD YOU RATHER...

...be able to read people's minds

OR

see their futures?

WOULD YOU RATHER...

...live with a really pongy smell for a day

OR

lose your sense of smell for a week?

WOULD YOU RATHER...

...have only 2 children in your class

OR

have 40 children in your class?

WOULD YOU RATHER...

...swallow a wriggly worm

OR

nibble a creepy caterpillar?

WOULD YOU RATHER...

...eat peas with a knife

OR

spaghetti sauce with a fork?

WOULD YOU RATHER...

...eat Brussels sprouts with honey for breakfast

OR

pancakes with mustard for dinner?

WOULD YOU RATHER...

...think that there are other intelligent lifeforms in the universe

OR

know for certain that we are the only ones?

WOULD YOU RATHER...

...be stuck on a desert island alone

OR

with someone who never stops talking?

WOULD YOU RATHER...

...give up brushing your teeth

OR

your hair?

WOULD YOU RATHER...

...be punished for something you didn't do

OR

let a friend take the blame for something bad you did?

WOULD YOU RATHER...

...live in never-ending summer

OR

never-ending winter?

WOULD YOU RATHER...

...forget how to read

OR

how to write?

WOULD YOU RATHER...

...see the same movie 20 times

OR

watch 20 different movies, but miss the last 20 minutes of each?

WOULD YOU RATHER...

...win

OR

take part?

WOULD YOU RATHER...

...meet 20 chicken-sized horses

OR

meet one horse-sized chicken?

WOULD YOU RATHER...

...end world hunger

OR

all wars forever?

QUICK FIRE QUESTIONS!

- front seat or back seat?
- milk or juice?
- ice-cream or ice-lolly?
- ocean or mountains?
- hot or cold?
- peas or carrots?
- top or bottom bunk?
- winter or summer?

QUICK FIRE QUESTIONS!

- bath or shower?
- early bird or night owl?
- kitten or puppy?
- scary or funny?
- cookie or apple?
- sit or stand?
- red or blue?
- forwards or backwards?

QUICK FIRE QUESTIONS!

- Monday or Friday?
- countryside or city?
- TV or book?
- burger or pizza?
- coloring or drawing?
- card game or video game?
- one friend or a crowd?
- Santa Claus or the Easter Bunny?

THINK OF SOME OF YOUR OWN!

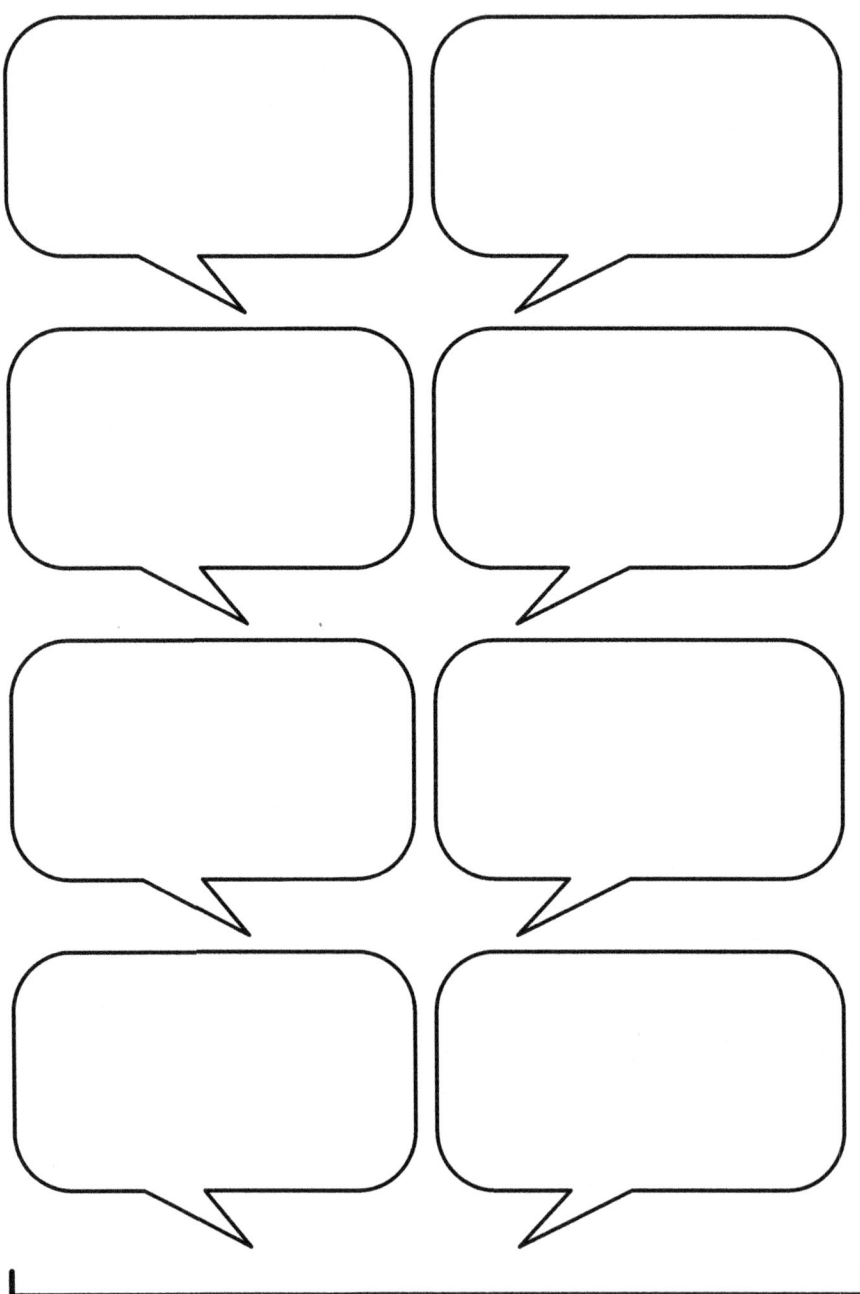

Printed in Dunstable, United Kingdom